Balkans Travel Guide 2024 and Beyond

A Journey Through Culture, Cuisine, and History

Henry Hardy

Table Of Contents

ENTRAL BALKAN REGION

INTRODUCTION TO THE BALKAN

My mind is filled with a kaleidoscope of memories, events, and feelings when I think of the Balkans. Situated in the southeast corner of Europe, the Balkans are an area rich in culture, history, and scenic beauty. Empires have come and gone across these territories, leaving a lasting legacy for both the environment and the people who live here.

I could sense the lingering remnants of bygone eras as I strolled through the narrow alleyways of historic cities like

Dubrovnik, Sarajevo, and Thessaloniki. This is the area where the East and the West converge, allowing you to cross from the colorful bazaars of a lively Ottoman town to the cobblestone alleyways of a medieval stronghold.

The Balkans are an expedition through the stories carved into the very stones underfoot; they are more than just a place to visit. Every step you take in the Balkans seems like you're turning a page in a live history book, from the medieval beauty of Bran Castle in Romania often associated with the Dracula legend to the jaw-dropping scenery of Plitvice Lakes National Park in Croatia, where waterfalls tumble through lush woods.

Cuisine is also quite important. A captivating mix of tastes characterizes the Balkan cuisine scene. You will have fragrant kebabs in Skopje's marketplaces, and the filling banitsa pastry is a must-try when in Bulgaria. A trip to this area wouldn't be complete without sampling cevapi, the Balkan equivalent of fast food a delicious mixture of minced meat served on fluffy pita bread.

The variety of the Balkans is among its most lovely features. From the dramatic mountains of Albania to the immaculate beaches of the Greek Islands, every nation and city has something special to offer. Examples of these include the bizarre beauty of Montenegro's Bay of Kotor. This is a place that appeals to history buffs and cultural vultures alike, as well as those who enjoy the outdoors and adventure.

But the people of the Balkans are what really make them unique. They are eager to share their history, customs, and hospitality with others. They are kind, hospitable, and intensely proud of their past. Lifelong friendships are frequently formed via conversations over homemade rakija or strong Turkish coffee.

Thus, as you get ready to travel across the Balkans, be ready to be astounded by its splendor, humbled by its past, and blessed by the kindness of its people.
Accompany me on this voyage as we explore the core of the Balkans, revealing the mysteries, myths, and marvels that render this area so alluring. We'll travel these meandering roads together, enjoy the cuisine, and appreciate the tales that have made the Balkans into the captivating place they are today. Welcome to the Balkans, a place where history, warmth, and adventure join together to create an unforgettable experience.

Cultural Diversity and Historical Significance

Greetings from the dynamic and alluring Balkans, in the heart of Europe, where you will discover a wealth of historical significance and cultural variety. This place is more than simply a place to visit; it's a voyage through time and civilizations that have forever changed the country and its inhabitants.

Cultural Diversity: The Balkans, a captivating fusion of cultures, customs, and languages, are tucked away in southeast Europe. You will come across an amazing fusion of Western and Eastern influences as you go through this fascinating area. You can see how various ethnic groups, faiths, and languages cohabit peacefully here. The Balkans are a live example of how civilizations are interwoven, from the Byzantine and Ottoman legacies to the Habsburg and Venetian imprints. Vibrant folk music, traditional dances, and a delicious culinary scene that differs by area are all part of the rich tapestry of cultural variety. Savor filling foods like cevapi, burek, moussaka, and baklava when traveling across the Balkans

Historical Significance: The Balkans have a rich history that dates back thousands of years. You will come across historical locations that have witnessed innumerable empires, conflicts, and significant periods in European history as you tour this region. Every region in the Balkans has a unique narrative to tell, from the ancient remains of Plovdiv to the majestic walls of Dubrovnik and the medieval charm of Sarajevo.
Explore the mysteries of the surviving Ottoman palaces, Byzantine basilicas, and Roman amphitheaters. The Balkans have a complicated history that includes conflicts in the 20th century, the rise and fall of empires, and fights for independence. Its past has influenced the people's tenacious and hospitable nature.

History in the Balkans is not limited to museums; it is there in the streets, in the voices of the people who live there, and in the beautiful architecture that adorns each city and hamlet.

Discover the famous Mostar Bridge in Bosnia and Herzegovina, a representation of resiliency and solidarity.

Explore the magnificent monasteries of Meteora in Greece or meander through the cobblestone alleyways of Ohrid, a UNESCO World Heritage site in North Macedonia. You are traveling through time with each step you take.
The Balkans offer an intensive journey into the depths of cultural variety and historical importance, not merely a place to visit. The tenacity, fervor, and genuineness of the area will linger long in your memory. Thus, enjoy the tastes of the Balkans, accept the kind welcome of the people, and let history's echoes lead you as you discover this fascinating region of the globe.

Geographical Features and Landscape

The Balkan Peninsula, which is tucked away in Southeast Europe, offers a breathtaking variety of scenery, from tranquil shores to imposing mountains.

Let's explore the geographical wonders that are in store for you.

Magnificent mountain chains
Soaring mountain ranges that offer an amazing background for your activities are often associated with the Balkans. Walking options abound in the ruggedly beautiful Dinaric Alps, which extend along the shore. Marvel at the verdant, lush surroundings as you explore Montenegro's Tara Canyon, one of the continent's deepest gorges.

The Rhodope Mountains, which stretch through Greece and Bulgaria to the east, are home to tranquil lakes, charming towns, and wooded woods. The hilly topography of the Balkans offers something for everyone, whether you're an enthusiastic hiker or just looking for peaceful nature.

Coastlines and Emerald Waters
Beach lovers will find bliss along the Adriatic and Ionian Sea coasts of the Balkans. The Dalmatian Coast of Croatia is a Mediterranean gem, including quaint old villages and pristine seas. Take a dive in the Adriatic and discover the secret coves and colorful underwater life.

The Riviera in Albania has a number of immaculate beaches that are frequently unspoiled by large crowds of people. You'll find pristine beauty wherever you look, from the sandy beaches of Ksamil to the relaxed vibe of Dhermi.

Lush Valleys and Plateaus: As one travels inland in the Balkans, one finds lush valleys and plateaus that are ideal for agriculture. Vojvodina in Serbia, with its enormous sunflower and wheat fields, is a perfect example. You will enjoy mouthwatering local goods and experience rural life in this area.

Mysterious Rivers and Lakes

There is an amazing variety of lakes and rivers throughout the Balkans. Croatia's Plitvice Lakes National Park is home to terraced lakes connected by wooden boardwalks and tumbling waterfalls. It's easy to understand why it's a UNESCO World Heritage site.

North Macedonia's Ohrid area is well-known for having one of Europe's oldest and deepest lakes, Lake Ohrid. It's a great place to go fishing and snorkeling because of its vibrant, clear seas.

Natural Wonders

Finally, don't overlook the Balkans' distinctive geological features. Vast cave systems may be found in Romania's Apuseni Mountains, while Slovenia's Postojna Cave is a fascinating subterranean world of stalactites and stalagmites.

You will be astounded by the sheer variety of geographical elements this region has to offer as you travel across the Balkans. Your vacation memories will be forever altered by the natural beauties of the Balkans, from their majestic peaks to their immaculate coasts and verdant valleys. The scenery of the Balkans is ready to be discovered and enjoyed, regardless of your interest in the great outdoors or your simple appreciation of the beauty of nature.

CHAPTER 1

PLANNING YOUR JOURNEY

Best Time to Visit the Balkans

Are you prepared to go off on an exciting journey that combines culture, history, and stunning scenery? Southeast

Europe's Balkans area provides a rich tapestry of experiences just waiting to be explored.
We'll help you plan your itinerary and choose the ideal time to visit this intriguing region of the world with our travel guide to the Balkans.

1. Select Your Trips: The Balkans are home to a number of states, each with its own character. Bosnia and Herzegovina, Greece, Croatia, and Montenegro are a few of the well-liked travel spots. Based on your interests, choose which nations and places to visit.

2. Trip Length: Take into account the amount of time you have available for your travel. Make sure to adjust your itinerary appropriately, as the Balkans may be a large and varied region. Whether your vacation is a few weeks or longer, make sure you leave enough time to experience each location to the fullest.

The ideal time to visit the Balkans might vary based on your tastes because the region experiences a variety of climates:

1. Spring (April to June): Traveling across the Balkans this season is pleasant. The scenery is verdant and lush, and the temperature is warm. Hiking, outdoor pursuits, and taking in the stunning Adriatic shoreline are all highly recommended.

2. Summer: The busiest travel season, particularly in coastal regions, is from July to August. Beach holidays and water activities are ideal due to the hot and sunny weather. But expect bigger people and more expensive pricing

3. Autumn (September to November): If you want more sedate settings and nice weather, autumn is an excellent time to come. For those who enjoy the outdoors, autumn is a lovely time of year because of how the leaves change color and alter the surroundings.

4. Winter (December to March): Although there may be snowfall and extreme cold in some Balkan regions at this time of year, winter may be a great time for those who enjoy winter sports. There are great prospects for skiing and snowboarding in countries like Serbia and Bulgaria.

The history, culture, and scenic beauty of the Balkans are alluring. You can make your trip to this fascinating area memorable and enlightening by carefully organizing your itinerary and picking the ideal time to come. The Balkans have something unique to offer, whether you're looking for adventure, leisure, or a combination of the two.

Entry Requirements and Visa Information

It's important to know the admission criteria for the Balkans before you set out on your tour. It's important to find out the particular criteria for the places you've decided to travel to because each country in the Balkans may have distinct regulations.

Here are a few typical factors to think about.

Validity of Passport: Verify that your passport is still valid six months after the date you want to leave the Balkans. It's advisable to err on the side of caution because different countries may have different criteria for passport validity.

Exemptions from the need for a visa: A few Balkan nations, including those in the European Union (such as Croatia, Slovenia, and Bulgaria), let visitors from specific nations enter for brief periods (sometimes up to 90 days) without a visa. Check to see whether any of these exemptions apply to you as a citizen.

Visa on Arrival: A few Balkan nations, such as Serbia, provide certain nationalities with a visa upon arrival. Make sure you are aware of the prerequisites, costs, and the maximum amount of time you may remain.

Schengen Area: The entrance and visa procedures for Balkan nations that are members of the Schengen Area, such as Slovenia, may be different from those of non-Schengen nations. Make careful to verify the rules for obtaining a visa before entering Schengen.

Details about Visas

The criteria for visas might differ greatly throughout Balkan countries. This is important for you to know:

Schengen Visa: If you want to go to any of the Schengen nations, including Slovenia, you should think about obtaining a Schengen Visa, which enables unrestricted movement inside the Schengen Area. The nation where you intend to spend the most time, or your initial destination if your time is equally divided, should be your entrance point into the Schengen Area.

Tourist Visas: Find out which countries in the Balkans that are not part of the Schengen area, such Serbia, Albania, and North Macedonia, require a visa. Depending on your country, you may need to apply ahead of time for a tourist visa. Usually, this entails submitting paperwork, making payments, and presenting your vacation itinerary.

E-Visas: You may apply online for e-visas in a few Balkan nations. In general, this procedure is quicker and more convenient than applying for a visa through traditional means.

Duration of stay: Verify how long you are allowed to remain according to the terms of your visa. There may be fines or other consequences for overstaying.

Supporting Documents: When applying for a visa, be ready to submit supporting documentation, such as a return ticket, proof of lodging, and travel insurance.

It's important to verify with the relevant embassies or consulates of the Balkan countries you want to visit for the most up-to-date information, as visa procedures and regulations are subject to change.

You will be well-prepared to see this varied and fascinating region if you take the time to learn about the entrance requirements and visa information for your trip to the Balkans.

Budgeting and Cost Considerations

Traveling to the Balkans is a thrilling trip that offers breathtaking scenery, a broad range of cultures, and a rich history. Here's a guide to help you manage your spending while experiencing this stunning region, whether you're a budget traveler, backpacker, or just someone who likes to get the most for their money.

1. **Lodging**: There are many different lodging alternatives in the Balkans to suit every budget. For the budget-conscious visitor, hostels, guesthouses, and cheap hotels are excellent options. While prices could differ from nation to nation, in general, you can find cozy accommodations for a small portion of what you might spend in Western Europe

2. **Food & Dining:** It's imperative to try the regional cuisine in the Balkans, and it may be reasonably priced as well. If you want to eat well without going over budget, look for neighborhood bakeries, eateries, and street food vendors. The cuisine of the Balkan countries is renowned for being filling and savory, and there are many affordable alternatives.

3. **Transportation:** Traveling between locations is easy because of the Balkan countries' excellent bus and train

networks. Compared to flying, these forms of transportation are frequently more affordable. Additionally, for short journeys, think about carpooling or other shared transportation choices like ride-sharing services.

4. Activities and Sightseeing: One of the best things about the Balkans is the abundance of reasonably priced or even free attractions, including historical landmarks, breathtaking natural formations, and cultural events. Profit from this and discover the breathtaking scenery and extensive history without breaking the bank.

5. Currency Exchange: Recognize that each country in the Balkans has its own currency and that they are not a part of the Eurozone. Learning about conversion rates and where to get the greatest deals is a smart idea. It is usually preferable to pay using local money, so be sure to have cash as well.

6. Shopping: The Balkans are a great place to get handcrafted goods and souvenirs. Despite the allure of shopping, keep an eye on your spending. Unique things may be found in local markets, but don't forget to bargain for a better price.

7. Travel Insurance: Think about getting travel insurance before you go on your vacation in the Balkans. If you make this tiny investment, you can avoid financial hardship and anxiety in the event of unforeseen circumstances such as flight delays, cancellations, or medical problems.

8. Make an Itinerary: Making an itinerary and planning ahead of time can help you keep costs down. Make a list of the places and things you want to do most, then budget your money appropriately. Doing ahead research might sometimes turn up exclusive offers and savings.

9. Off-Peak Travel: Since lodging and airfare might be less expensive during shoulder seasons or off-peak periods, take this into consideration. You may also have a better time when there are less people around.

You will have an amazing trip in the Balkans without breaking the bank. You can make your journey to this fascinating area both memorable and reasonably priced by keeping an eye on your spending, looking for choices that fit within your budget, and making advance plans. The magnificent Adriatic coast, the ancient towns, or the charming countryside are what entice travelers on a tight budget to visit the Balkans.

CHAPTER 2

NAVIGATING THE BALKANS

Transportation Options within the Region

The Balkans are a region with a wide range of topography, cultural traditions, and historical events. It's an adventure in and of itself to navigate this breathtaking region of the planet.

We'll assist you in learning the finest routes around this intriguing area in our travel guide.
With the diversity of nations and landscapes that make up the Balkans, it is important to have a range of transportation alternatives available to you.

Here's how to navigate this fascinating region of Europe

Trains: Traveling in the Balkans is both picturesque and reasonably priced thanks to the region's well-connected train network. Major towns including Belgrade, Zagreb, Sofia, and Thessaloniki are connected by trains, which offer a chance to see the stunning landscape. The renowned "Balkan Flexipass" provides excellent flexibility for several rail trips around the region.

Buses: Buses are a common mode of transportation for getting between smaller towns and areas that might not have train connections. Numerous bus companies have lines that wind across the Balkans, making it simple to get to even the most isolated locations.

Ferries: Because the Balkans are close to the Adriatic, Ionian, and Aegean Seas, taking a ferry voyage is an experience as much as a means of transportation. Take a boat ride to discover the breathtaking islands and coasts of Greece, Montenegro, and Croatia.

Car Rentals: Hiring a car is a great choice if you're the independent and flexible kind. The Balkans provide for beautiful driving destinations, and if you have your own car, you might discover hidden treasures that might be difficult to reach by public transportation.

Domestic planes: When flying between large cities, domestic planes can reduce time, even if railroads and buses are still a realistic option for most travels. Prices and availability might change based on the route, so be sure to check.

Taxis and Ride-Sharing: For short trips inside cities, ride-sharing services like Uber and taxis are practical options. They provide easy access to nearby attractions and navigation around cities.

Walking and Cycling: For the more daring tourists, these are two excellent modes of transportation for exploring both the countryside and the towns. There are bike-sharing programs in many cities, and hiking routes with breathtaking views of the Balkans' natural beauty may be found there.

Public Transportation: Public transportation is economical and effective in places like Athens, Sofia, and Belgrade. Make easy use of the metro, buses, and trams to navigate the city.

Border Crossings: Be aware that certain border crossings in the Balkans may need additional paperwork and time, so research the entrance procedures for each country you intend to visit in advance and be ready.

As you travel across the Balkans, you'll come across an area that offers an intriguing blend of history, landscapes, and cultures. Whichever way you choose to go, every trip is an adventure to discover the undiscovered beauties of this unique region of Europe. Happy travels!

Tips for Efficient Travel Between Countries

While every Balkan nation has its own distinct appeal, getting the most out of your trip depends on how well you can navigate between these varied locations.
We've included some priceless advice in this Balkans travel guide to help you navigate between these intriguing nations with ease.

1. **Make Your Travel Schedule**: There are many nations to visit in the Balkans, which is a varied region. Make a rough schedule of the countries you want to visit and the things you want to see in each before you go. This will guarantee that you don't miss any must-see places and help you make the most of your stay.

2. **Verify Visa Requirements**: The prerequisites for obtaining a visa differ throughout Balkan nations and are subject to alter. Make sure you read up on and comprehend the visa requirements in each nation you want to visit. You may be able to travel between several Balkan nations with a Schengen visa, much like you can travel between some EU countries.

3. **Currency Considerations:** Different countries may have different currencies. Some Balkan countries have their own currencies, while others utilize the Euro. Having access to ATMs or carrying some local cash is a smart idea, especially if you want to visit more isolated locations.

4. Knowledge of the Local Language: Although English is the primary language in most large cities, knowing the basics of the local tongue may be quite beneficial, particularly in rural regions. Gaining some common language proficiency will greatly improve your trip experience.

5**. transit Option**s: Buses, trains, and airplanes are all part of the well-connected transit networks in the Balkans. Look into your alternatives and reserve seats in advance on busy routes. Bus travel is a popular and reasonably priced mode of transportation that lets you take in the area's natural beauty.

6. Border Crossings: Be advised that the paperwork and customs inspections at several Balkan border crossings might make the process lengthy. Be patient and allow this to factor into your trip time.7. Venture Off the trodden road: Although major cities like Sofia, Athens, and Belgrade are amazing, don't forget to go off the trodden road. The Balkans are full with undiscovered treasures, from idyllic towns to immaculate coastlines. Seize the chance to see less-traveled locations.

8. Sample Local Food: Foodies will love the Balkan cuisine. In every nation you visit, make sure to sample the native cuisine, such as cevapi, moussaka, and burek. It's a great way to engage with the local way of life.

9. Honor Local Traditions: Each Balkan nation has its own traditions and customs. Be kind and educate yourself about regional manners. This will improve your communication with the people and add special memories to your trip.

10.Travel Insurance: Lastly, but just as importantly, never undervalue its significance. Make sure you have enough insurance to cover unforeseen circumstances, such as lost luggage or medical problems.

A voyage through history, culture, and magnificent scenery is what it means to explore the Balkans. By keeping these pointers in mind, you'll be ready to set out on an amazing journey. Prepare yourself for a unique travel experience as you explore the Balkans!

Must-See Landmarks and Historical Sites

Discovering the fascinating Balkans will show you immediately what a wealth of history, culture, and varied landscapes the area has to offer. There are several must-see monuments and historical attractions to include in your vacation itinerary, ranging from medieval fortifications situated on precipitous cliffs to quaint little towns that have lasted decades.

1. Croatia's Dubrovnik

The Adriatic Pearl Known as the "Pearl of the Adriatic," Dubrovnik is a stunningly maintained medieval city. Magnificent views of the Adriatic Sea may be had from its well-known city walls, which date back to the seventh century. Take a stroll along the Stradun, pay a visit to the Rector's Palace, and become lost in this UNESCO World Heritage Sites rich past.

2. Croatia's Plitvice Lakes National Park

A kaleidoscope of blue lakes, waterfalls, and lush flora, Plitvice Lakes National Park is a UNESCO-listed natural treasure. Experience the enchantment of this natural environment by taking a stroll along the wooden boardwalks.

3. Bled, Slovenia: Island and Fairytale Castle

Bled, with its idyllic lake, is home to a little island with a chapel on it and a medieval castle built on a hill. In addition to riding the traditional boat, you may visit the castle and ring the wishing bell on the island.

4. The Stari Most Bridge in Mostar, Bosnia and Herzegovina

The Stari Most Bridge in Mostar is a testament to architectural beauty as well as a symbol of resiliency and solidarity. Enjoy the captivating views and see the daredevils leaping into the Neretva River from the bridge.

5. **The Acropolis in Athens, Greece**

Athens' Acropolis serves as a reminder of the architectural and cultural grandeur of classical Greece. Explore the Parthenon, Erechtheion, and Propylaea, and be amazed at where democracy originated.

6. Topkapi Palace and Hagia Sophia in Istanbul, Turkey

See the Hagia Sophia, which has functioned as both a church and a mosque, and then visit the Topkapi Palace, which is home to exquisite relics from bygone eras, to learn more about the rich history of the Ottoman Empire.

7. Split, Croatia: Palace of Diocletian

Enter the walls of Split's Diocletian's Palace and travel through time. You may stroll around its winding alleyways, take in the stunning Roman architecture, and take in the lively ambiance of this living historical monument.

8. Kotor, The Walled City of Montenegro

Encircled by imposing city walls, Kotor's ancient town is a labyrinth of cobblestone alleyways and quaint squares. Explore the city's historic churches and palaces and climb the city walls for a breathtaking perspective of the bay.

9. Kalemegdan Fortress in Belgrade, Serbia

A historical treasure, Kalemegdan Fortress offers sweeping vistas of the Danube and Sava rivers coming together. To learn about Serbia's past, take a stroll through the park, stop at the fortress, and browse the Military Museum.

10. Plovdiv, Bulgaria: Historic Old Town and Ancient Theatre

One of the oldest cities in Europe, Plovdiv has a beautifully preserved Roman amphitheater as well as a quaint old town with cobblestone lanes and colorful homes. Savor the fusion of the old and the new in this alluring metropolis.

The historical sites and landmarks of the Balkans provide insight into the region's rich and complicated past. Discovering these alluring locations will leave you really appreciating the cultural mosaic that makes the Balkans so remarkable in addition to being in awe of their beauty.

Natural Wonders and Scenic Beauty

Together, let's take a tour of some of this magical region of the world's most astounding natural beauties and picturesque settings.

1. Plitvice Lakes, Croatia:

The magnificent Plitvice Lakes National Park in Croatia is the first stop on our tour. Nestled among verdant woodlands, this UNESCO World Heritage site has a sequence of tiered lakes and tumbling waterfalls. You will be enthralled with the glistening clean waters as you stroll over wooden boardwalks, which shift in color according to the direction of the light.

2. Tara River Canyon, Montenegro

This is a must-see location for adventure lovers in Montenegro. This is one of Europe's deepest valleys and provides exhilarating white-water rafting adventures. The lush forests, sheer cliffs, and green waterways provide for a breathtaking backdrop for this exhilarating journey.

3. Rila Monastery and Seven Rila Lakes, Bulgaria

Take in the tranquil splendor of this cultural treasure, the calm Rila Monastery, which is encircled by the breathtaking Seven Rila Lakes. Nestled in the serene and ethereal Rila Mountains, these lakes offer an ideal setting for trekking and taking pictures.

4. Kotor Bay, Montenegro

Known as Europe's southernmost fjord, the Bay of Kotor is an amazing inlet encircled by high rocks. The views from Kotor's city walls are breathtaking, and the old town is recognized as a UNESCO World Heritage site.

5. **Lake Ohrid, North Macedonia**

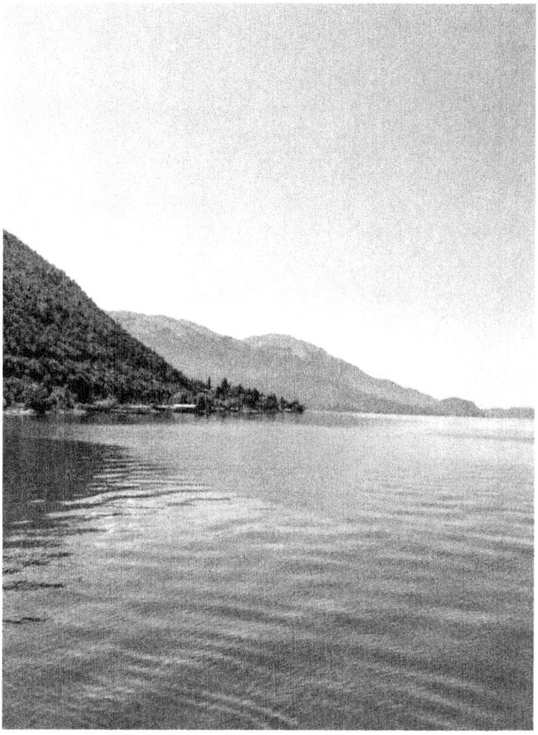

Regarded as the "Pearl of the Balkans," this lake is among Europe's oldest and deepest. It's the perfect place for leisure and adventure because of its crystal-clear seas, gorgeous beaches, and quaint lakeside villages.

6. Durmitor National Park, Montenegro

This UNESCO-listed park is a haven for hikers and environment lovers, including magnificent peaks, glistening glacial lakes, and thick woods. Specifically, the Black Lake is a charming location for a leisurely stroll or a quiet picnic.

7. Paklenica National Park, Croatia

Paklenica National Park is a climber's paradise if you enjoy looking at rock formations. The breathtaking canyons and high limestone cliffs make it the perfect place for outdoor activities like hiking and rock climbing.

8. Vikos Gorge, Greece

Lastly, our tour wouldn't be complete without a mention of Greece's Vikos Gorge. One of the world's deepest gorges, it provides breathtaking vistas, hiking paths, and an opportunity to experience the unspoiled splendor of the natural environment.

These are only a handful of the many amazing views you'll see in this gorgeous region of the Balkans, which is a natural wonderland just waiting to be explored. The Balkans have something to offer everyone, whether they are history buffs, adventure seekers, or just those looking for peace and quiet in the great outdoors. So gather your belongings and get ready to be mesmerized by the breathtaking scenery that this enchanted region of Europe has to offer.

Architectural Marvels and Cultural Centers

We'll take you on a tour of the architectural marvels and cultural hubs that make the Balkans a treasure awaiting discovery in this travel guide.

Amazing Buildings

Turkey's Hagia Sophia in Istanbul The Hagia Sophia, a representation of the Byzantine and Ottoman empires, is a great place to start your architectural exploration. You will be in awe of this masterpiece's combination of exquisite mosaics, breathtaking domes, and a fascinating past.

Croatia's Dubrovnik Old Town

Take a tour of the immaculately restored city walls of this "Pearl of the Adriatic." Its picturesque squares, historic architecture, and the stunning views of the Adriatic Sea will fascinate you.

Greece's Meteora Monasteries

These monasteries, perched on massive granite columns, are symbols of human devotion and inventiveness. This place is a marvel of natural and architectural harmony.

North Macedonia's main city, Skopje

North Macedonia's main city, Skopje: has undergone an intriguing metamorphosis. Numerous neoclassical structures, monuments, and bridges honoring the nation's past and culture can be seen in Skopje.

Cultural Hubs
Sarajevo, Bosnia and Herzegovina

Take in the city's many cultural offerings. Explore the old Baščaršija marketplace, which combines elements of Yugoslav, Austro-Hungarian, and Ottoman cultures.

Belgrade, Serbia

With its museums, theaters, and galleries, Serbia's capital is a thriving center of the arts. A look into the past of the city and breathtaking vistas may be found at Kalemegdan Fortress.

Greece's Thessaloniki

This is home to several museums, including the Museum of Byzantine Culture and the Archaeological Museum, which showcase the city's cultural richness. Don't forget to examine the city's emblem, the White Tower.

Ohrid, North Macedonia, is home to several churches, notably the Church of St. John at Kaneo, which has a view of Lake Ohrid. Ohrid is well-known for its intact medieval old town.

The Balkans provide an intriguing fusion of architectural wonders, cultural variety, and historical legacy. The Balkans have a lot to offer anybody interested in architecture, history, or just having rich cultural experiences.

CHAPTER 3

IMMERSING IN LOCAL CULTURE

Unique Traditions and Festivals

Traveling through the captivating landscapes and energetic towns of the Balkans will reveal that this fascinating region offers much more than simply breathtaking scenery and important historical sites. It's also a region with many festivals and deeply ingrained customs, providing you with a fantastic chance to fully immerse yourself in the diverse tapestry of Balkan culture. Let's investigate some distinctive customs and celebrations that will awe you and let you feel as though you are in the Balkans.

1. **Bulgaria's Kukeri Festival:** One of the country's most notable customs is the Kukeri Festival. Imagine individuals dressed in magnificent, colorful costumes depicting mythological animals with large masks on their heads. The intention? to ward off bad spirits and guarantee an abundant crop. A captivating show that captures the traditional rites and beliefs of the Balkans is produced by the lively dancing and the rhythmic jingling of bells.

2. **Međimurje Wine Festival (Croatia)**: Međimurje Wine Festival is a monument to the Balkans' renowned winemaking heritage. Locals and visitors gather for this Croatian festivity to savor the produce of the vineyards. Enjoy traditional music, sample a range of wines, and take part in toasts that stand for harmony and friendship.

3. **Bobrek Bread Festival (North Macedonia):** Held in the town of Kratovo, this event honors the long-standing custom of baking bread together. Together, the local bakers create a large loaf as a sign of wealth and harmony. You may sample this unique bread and discover the cultural significance it has for the neighborhood.

4. **Đurđevdan (Serbia):** This May 6th celebration is an Orthodox Serbian feast entwined with customs and traditions.

At churches and monasteries, people congregate to burn candles and make wishes. In addition, there will be folk music, dancing, and mouthwatering traditional cuisine, such as lamb that has been grilled on a spit.

5. Albanian Bektashi Order Gathering: A distinct presence in the Balkans, the Bektashi Order is a Sufi order. Each year on the birthday of the founder, Haji Bektash Veli, devotees and inquisitive tourists congregate at the Bektashi Tekke in Krujë. It's a time for sharing meals, dancing, and indulging in exciting music as well as spiritual thought.

Experiencing the warmth and generosity of the locals while taking part in these remarkable customs is what it means to fully immerse oneself in local culture in the Balkans. For a very genuine and remarkable experience, plan your exploration of this fascinating area to coincide with one of these distinctive events. The people of the Balkans are eager to welcome you and share their rich cultural traditions with you.

Cultural Etiquette and Social Customs

It's crucial to be aware of social norms and cultural etiquette before you set out on your tour through these fascinating countries in order to guarantee a courteous and easy travel experience.

This is a helpful handbook to help you travel the Balkans with understanding and grace.

Warm Greetings: In the Balkans, especially when friends and family are involved, greetings are frequently warm and include a peck on both cheeks. It is customary to shake hands firmly in formal settings. Until asked to use first names, it is common to address new acquaintances using titles such as "Mr." or "Mrs."

Although welcomes are heartfelt, remember to respect others' personal space. It's normal to stand closer than you may in certain Western countries in busy areas. This is not an indication of intrusion, but rather of friendship.

Table manners: Since food plays a major role in Balkan culture, you'll probably find yourself enjoying delectable meals with the locals. When eating, do not sip anything until the host makes the first toast and begins the meal. Completing your plate indicates gratitude for the food and is considered courteous. Please feel free to give the chef praise!

Dress with decency

It is customary to dress conservatively in certain regions of the Balkans, especially while visiting places of worship. On the other hand, seaside regions might be more laid back. When visiting places of worship, it's a good idea to have a scarf or shawl with you so you may cover your head and shoulders.

Giving Gifts

It's considerate to bring a modest gift for your host or from your own nation. Gifts like flowers, chocolates, or mementos are frequently valued. Show respect by using both hands while offering a gift.

Language and Communication: Slavic, Romance, and Albanian languages are spoken across the Balkans, which have a diverse linguistic population. Although most people in metropolitan areas speak English, knowing a few simple words in the local tongue might help you establish rapport.

Recognize Local Traditions: It's a good idea to investigate the traditions and customs of the Balkan countries before visiting, as each one has its own unique set. Whether you're celebrating St. Ivan's Day in Bulgaria or Orthodox Easter in Serbia, getting to know and honoring these regional customs can make your trip more enjoyable.

Life Expectancy: People in the Balkans typically lead more carefree lives. If anything takes a little longer than anticipated, don't be alarmed. Seize the chance to take things slowly and enjoy the present.

Tipping: Although customs around tipping differ, it's usually accepted. Tipping 10–15% of the bill or rounding up is standard at restaurants. It's wise to make sure that a service charge hasn't been applied previously.

You will have a more genuine and immersive experience in the Balkans and demonstrate respect for the locals and their customs by adhering to these social mores and cultural etiquette. The Balkans are a historical and hospitality hotspot, and they would appreciate your grasp of their traditions. So go forth smiling and with an open heart, and let the Balkans' natural beauty and its people charm you.

Arts, Music, and Folklore of the Balkans

Traveling across the Balkans' beautiful landscapes and varied civilizations will quickly reveal to you this region's wealth of creative expression, soul-stirring music, and enthralling folklore. With the help of our Balkans travel guide, you are cordially invited to discover the culture, music, and traditions that have molded this extraordinary region of the globe.

A Thousand Stories in One Piece of Art

Balkan art is a reflection of the turbulent past and dynamic present, with a strong historical and traditional foundation. Art comes in a multitude of shapes and forms that tell the tales of bygone eras, from the exquisite hand-woven carpets of Albania to the captivating murals that grace Serbian Orthodox monasteries.

1. Traditional Crafts: Local artists still employ age-old methods to create exquisite woodworking, textiles, and pottery. Not only are these handcrafted customs stunning, but they also serve as a reminder of the region's rich cultural legacy.

2. Iconic Frescoes: Churches and monasteries throughout the Balkans are home to magnificent frescoes and icons that are part of a great legacy of religious art. Serb monasteries such as Gračanica and Studenica provide witness to the talent and dedication of these artisans.

3. Contemporary Art Scenes: Showcasing the contemporary side of Balkan culture, capital towns like Belgrade, Sofia, and Zagreb are teeming with galleries and colorful street art.
Soundtracks that Inspire

The Balkans rely heavily on their music. Ancient villages, city squares, and even isolated mountainous areas may all hear it. The region's many musical traditions clearly reflect the harmonious blending of Eastern and Western influences.

1. Folk Music: The mournful sevdalinka of Bosnia and Herzegovina and the upbeat kolo dance melodies of Serbia are just two examples of the engaging folk music that the Balkans are known for. These tunes are the lifeblood of regional festivities.

2. Romani Music: The blazing sounds of Romani brass bands and the impassioned vocals of Romani singers have left a lasting impression on Balkan music.

3. Contemporary Fusion: Artists such as Goran Bregović have created compelling and electrifying music by skillfully fusing current and traditional Balkan sounds.

Traditions are given life by folklore

The intriguing fabric of myths, traditions, and superstitions that have been passed down through the ages makes up Balkan folklore. Numerous celebrations are held in honor of the rich cultural fabric that these legends have constructed.

1. Festivals and Celebrations: Take in the spirit and meaning of regional celebrations such as Bulgaria's Kukeri or Hungary and Croatia's Busójárás masquerade customs. These celebrations bring folklore to life via colorful dance, music, and costumes.

2. Mythical Creatures: The Balkans are home to a multitude of mythical creatures, ranging from the enigmatic Romanian vampires to the mystical creatures in Slavic mythology.
The Balkans are a voyage into the core of creative expression, musical resonance, and ancient folklore rather than merely a place to visit.

Discovering the historic frescoes of a Serbian monastery, swaying to the beats of a Romanian gypsy band, or immersing yourself in the legends of legendary creatures and the arts, music, and culture of the Balkans will make a lasting impression on your spirit.
Accept the vibrant cultural fabric of this captivating area, where each touch of music, tale, and brushstroke bears witness to its timeless essence.

CHAPTER 4

OFF THE BEATEN PATH

Hidden Gems and Undiscovered Destinations

The Balkans are a place of rich histories and various cultures; they are not just about well-traveled routes; they also have a

wealth of unexplored areas and hidden jewels just waiting to be discovered.
So let's set off on an adventure to discover the hidden gems of the Balkans off the main track.

1. North Macedonia's Matka Canyon's Magic:
A well-kept secret among residents, Matka Canyon is a gorgeous natural refuge tucked away just outside of Skopje, the capital. Hike along scenic paths, see historic caverns, and take a boat ride on the green waters of the Treska River. Matka Canyon is a peaceful haven from the hustle and bustle of the city.

2. Montenegro's Unspoiled Beauty of Kotor: Although the Bay of Kotor is well-known, venture past the bustling old town. The little towns of Prcanj and Perast are home to breathtaking views and ancient charm. Take in the breath-taking views from the less frequented St. John's Fortress summit.

3. The Mysterious North Macedonia's Pelister National Park is located close to the town of Bitola, where it is easily overlooked. It is a paradise with unique plants, glacial lakes, and thick woods. For those who enjoy the outdoors and hiking, the high-altitude routes are ideal.

4. Hidden Tranquility at Rila Monastery, Bulgaria: Although the monastery is well-known, not many visitors explore the nearby mountains. Discover the area's calm beauty and spirituality by strolling among the paths and secret churches.

5. The Adorable Village of Mostar, Bosnia and Herzegovina: Mostar is well-known for its bridge, but if you venture into the nearby hills, you'll find quaint communities like Blagaj. This is the location of the Buna River Spring, a secret haven where a cave produces azure waters.

6. Discovering the Albanian Riviera: Leave the congested beaches behind and travel the Albanian Riviera south. There are unspoiled coves, undiscovered beaches, and genuine fishing communities like Dhermi where you may sample the regional food and culture.

7. The Subterranean World of Demir Baba Teke, Bulgaria: Explore the enigmatic passageways and subterranean tunnels beneath the shrine dedicated to Demir Baba Teke. Only a select few tourists are able to take advantage of this unusual and fascinating encounter.

Getting off the main path in the Balkans may open your eyes and give you a deeper understanding of this very culturally varied region. Keep in mind to respect local customs and traditions as you discover these hidden treasures and unexplored sites, leaving no trace other than your admiration for the beauty you encounter.

Rural Escapes and Authentic Village Life

The gorgeous coasts and charming cities are frequently the main draws when it comes to traveling around the Balkans. However, the allure of rural getaways and real village life is a different type of treasure that is waiting to be found, buried away from the busy city streets and popular tourist destinations.

A Trip Through Time: Envision meandering roads guiding you through verdant, verdant settings where it appears as though time has stopped. Nestled amid the charming villages that dot the landscape, this is where you'll find the heart and soul of the Balkans.
These rural getaways are beautiful because they provide an insight into a slower-paced, more traditional way of life where community and simplicity are the core characteristics.

Take in the genuineness: One of the most amazing things about the rural Balkans is how you are surrounded by genuineness. Upon entering these towns, you will be welcomed with kind grins from residents who are excited to share their rituals, tales, and home-cooked treats. You will undoubtedly be greeted like a long-lost friend wherever you go whether it's the bucolic countryside of Bulgaria, the tranquil villages of Bosnia and Herzegovina, or the rugged landscape of Montenegro.

The Experience of Rural Balkans: Traveling through these areas is similar to traveling through time. Engaging in activities such as tending to vineyards, making bread in traditional ovens, or even taking part in the ancient art of beekeeping will be available to you. Hiking routes crisscross the countryside, catering to those with an adventurous spirit who want to experience nature at its most pristine. These trails lead to quiet locations and secret waterfalls.

Culinary Delights: The kitchen is the center of the household in these settlements. One of the best things about rural Balkan cuisine is the fresh, local ingredients used in its recipes. Savor delectable grilled meats, stews, and pies, sometimes served with homemade wine or rakija. Enjoy some freshly baked bread and local cheeses; they make for memorable and rustic dining experiences.

Where to Start: Areas like Istria in Croatia, the Rhodope Mountains in Bulgaria, and the Albanian Alps provide some of the most alluring rural getaways in the Balkans. Every town has a distinct personality and tale to share, which makes it a worthwhile trip of discovery and cultural immersion.

When you travel around the Balkans, think about going outside the popular tourist areas to get a true taste of rural life. It's an opportunity to take it slowly, appreciate the present, and make memories that you'll carry with you for a very long time. So gather your belongings, get off the main track, and see the unspoiled beauty of the rural Balkans. You will be rewarded with one of the most authentic travel experiences possible.

Lesser-Known Natural Reserves and Parks

While many tourists go to well-known locations in this region of the world, there are undiscovered gems awaiting exploration, such as lesser-known parks and natural reserves that provide a distinctive, unspoiled experience. We'll share some of these undiscovered treasures with you in our Balkans travel guide, so bring out your inner nature lover.

1. Montenegro's Biogradska Gora National Park:
The pristine Biogradska Gora National Park is tucked away in the center of Montenegro. One of the few remaining rainforests in Europe, Biogradsko Lake is surrounded by old woods in this park. Hike along paths, see a variety of species, and take in the clean mountain air.

2. Bulgaria's Bistrishko Branishte: This lesser-known nature reserve has a distinct appeal and is tucked away in the Rila Mountains. Hikers and nature lovers will find paradise here as they stroll through it verdant forests, take in the beauty of glacial lakes, and take in the peace and quiet of a far-off place.

3.Tara National Park, Serbia: Although its neighbor, Durmitor National Park in Montenegro, receives a lot of publicity, Tara National Park in Serbia is still a little-known treasure. This park is well-known for the pure Drina River, its deep gorges, and its untamed scenery. Popular activities here include bird viewing, hiking, and rafting

4. Galicica National Park, North Macedonia: This park, which is sandwiched between Lake Ohrid and Lake Prespa, is frequently eclipsed by its well-known surrounding lakes. On the other hand, this park has several hiking and mountain biking paths, as well as a wide variety of plants and animals.

5. Theth National Park, Albania: Nestled in the Albanian Alps, Theth National Park is a veritable hidden gem. Trekkers and intrepid travelers looking for an off-the-beaten-path experience will find it to be the perfect location because of its secluded settlements, breathtaking waterfalls, and steep terrain.

6. Orjen, Montenegro: Known for its breathtaking scenery of verdant woods, rugged cliffs, and secret caverns, Orjen is one of Europe's lesser-known massifs. For people who like to hike and discover interesting geological formations, it's an excellent location.

Prepare to become completely immersed in nature, away from the throng, and discover the undiscovered beauty of the Balkans when you visit these lesser-known parks and natural reserves nearby.
These locations offer a sense of peace and an opportunity to commune with nature that are sometimes difficult to discover in busier tourist areas. These undiscovered treasures in the Balkans will leave you with priceless memories of the area's natural beauties, regardless of your interests, adventure, wildlife, or just a love of the great outdoors.

CHAPTER 5

GASTRONOMIC DELIGHTS

Iconic Balkan Dishes and Local Cuisine

The Balkan culinary scene is a treasure trove of tastes just waiting to be discovered, from substantial soups to exquisite kebabs. We'll take you on a gastronomic adventure via 10 signature dishes and the diverse regional cuisine that characterizes the Balkans in this travel guide.

1. Cevapi (Ćevapi)

A popular meal in the Balkans, these little grilled sausages are usually cooked with a mixture of beef and lamb. They are eaten with chopped onions, kajmak, a creamy dairy spread, and pita-like bread.

2. Burek

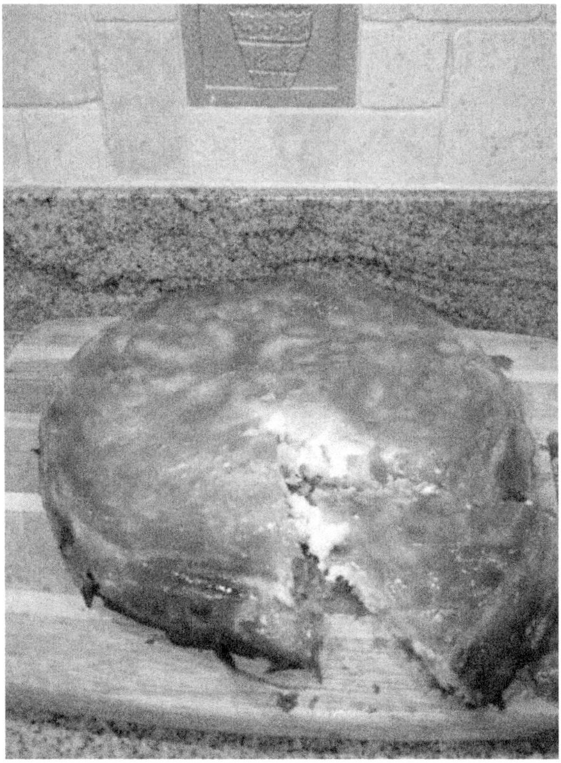

A mainstay of Balkan street cuisine, burek is a flaky pastry stuffed with a variety of ingredients including cheese, minced meat, or spinach. It's ideal for a simple, flavorful snack.

3. Pljeskavica

Also known as the Balkan burger, is a delicious beef patty that is often served with a variety of toppings and sauces. Try it with the red pepper-based sauce called ajvar.

4. Sarma

Served with a side of yogurt, sarma is a dish of perfectly cooked ground pork, rice, and spices packed within cabbage leaves. It is the epitome of comfort food.

5. Ajvar

Made from roasted red peppers, eggplant, and garlic, ajvar is a tasty condiment but not a meal in and of itself. It goes well with bread, meat, or anything that needs a taste explosion.

6. Goulash

Served over mashed potatoes or noodles, Balkan goulash is a substantial stew composed with soft pieces of meat, typically pig or beef, simmered with onions and paprika.

7. Moussaka

A layered meal of minced beef, eggplant, and a thick béchamel sauce, moussaka is a Balkan take on a traditional dish. Every area adds a special touch to this hearty meal.

8. Rakia

A traditional Balkan fruit brandy with strong potency. To truly experience the nuances of the region, try rakia with different fruit flavors like plum, grape, or pear.

9. Peka

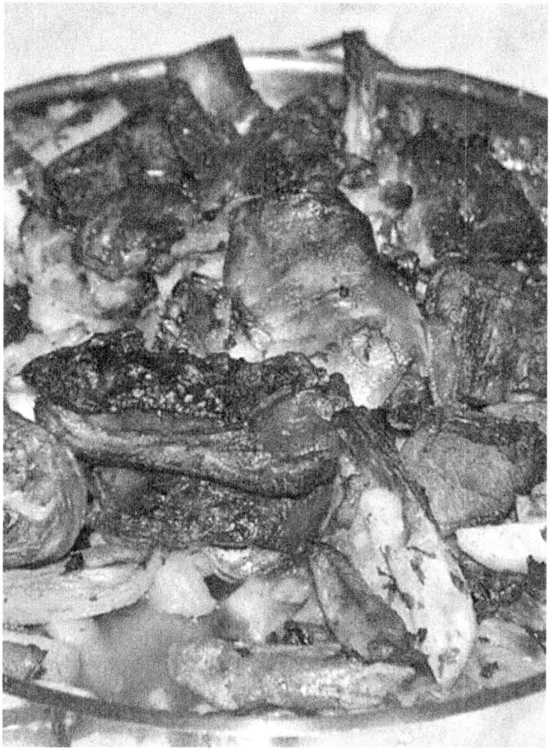

A one-pot wonder that cooks slowly, is a mixture of meat and vegetables that are baked with a bell-shaped lid after being drizzled with olive oil and herbs.

10.Conclude your Balkan gastronomic adventure with a delightful treat known as baklava.

This exquisite pastry is crafted by layering thin sheets of phyllo dough with nuts and a generous drizzle of sweet syrup, and it enjoys widespread adoration as a beloved dessert across the region.

Savor these well-known foods and celebrate the gastronomic diversity of the Balkans while you go there. The Balkans provide an array of sensations that will satisfy your palate and your heart, from the busy streets of Belgrade to the mountainous landscape of Montenegro.

Top-Rated Restaurants and Culinary Experiences

You are in for an unparalleled gastronomic experience when it comes to the Balkans. There are many highly regarded eateries and culinary experiences in this multicultural region, which includes nations like Bosnia and Herzegovina, Croatia, Serbia, and more, to suit a range of palates.

1. Cevapi's Savory Treats in Bosnia & Herzegovina: Begin your gastronomic exploration of the Balkans in Bosnia and Herzegovina with the popular meal Cevapi, which is made of minced meat (usually lamb or beef) shaped into little sausages and cooked to perfection. This meal is a must-try, served with fresh bread, onions, and a dollop of kajmak, a creamy dairy spread. Visit neighborhood eateries to savor this traditional Balkan dish.

2. Croatian Seafood Extravaganza: Croatia is a seafood lover's heaven. Great fish restaurants can be found in abundance in coastal cities like Split and Dubrovnik. Savor delectable dishes like grilled fish and octopus salad, all while taking in breathtaking views of the Adriatic Sea.

3. Serbian Grilled Meats & Pljeskavica: Pljeskavica, a burger-like patty prepared from a mixture of ground meats, is a particularly delicious meal from Serbia, which is well-known for its grilled meats. It's a carnivore's dream, served in a fresh (flatbread) with an assortment of toppings. In Belgrade and around the nation, neighborhood grill establishments are well-known for their sizzling .

4. Albanian Byrek and Local Taverns: The country is well-known for its delicious pastry stuffed with meat, cheese, or spinach. Discover the neighborhood bakeries and bars to enjoy this warming delicacy, which is often best had with a potent Albanian coffee.

5. Macedonian Ajvar and the Flavor of **Tradition**: Dishes like the red pepper-based condiment Ajvar provide a flavor of tradition. To taste the flavors of Macedonian cuisine, which frequently consists of hearty stews, grilled meats, and fresh veggies, visit neighborhood markets and eateries.

6. Montenegrin Black Risotto: Made with squid ink, this dish from Montenegro offers a distinctive take on shellfish. This meal, which comes with a variety of seafood, is quite tasty and visually arresting. Kotor and Budva, two coastal towns, are great places to savor this treat.

7. Craft Beer in the Balkans: There is a resurgence of craft beer in the Balkans for people who enjoy a fine brew. Local breweries in the region, especially in towns like Zagreb (Croatia), Ljubljana (Slovenia), and Belgrade, provide a great assortment of craft beers to go with your meals.

The Balkans provide something for everyone's taste buds, whether you're an adventurous eater, a fan of traditional foods, or a traveler seeking for new delicacies. A voyage for both your taste senses and your spirit, the region's rich and varied gastronomic tapestry is a monument to the cultural legacy of each nation. So, one dish at a time, absorb the flavors, take in the atmosphere, and celebrate the Balkans.

Traditional Drinks and Regional Specialties

An example of what to anticipate is as follows:

Customary Drinks

The powerful fruit brandy known as Rakia (Rakija) is the pride of the Balkans. It is available in apricot, grape, and plum flavors, among other fruit flavors. Whether it's for a cold or

HOTEL OTRANT
★ ★ ★ ★

UPLATA TURISTIČKE TAKSE I OSIGURANJE

Datum: . .20

BROJ SOBE	205

PERIOD BORAVKA DAN	04.05 05.05.

RB.	*Ime i prezime gosta*	*Broj Dana*	*Cijena / Dan*	*Iznos*
1	2x2,50	1		5,00
2				
3				
4				
5				
6				
7				
8				
	UKUPNO			5,00

Potpis Gosta

Ovjera Recepcije

PERIOD BORAVKA	05.05
DAN	05.05

just to have a toast with friends, the locals frequently see it as the panacea.

Raki

Well-liked in Albania and Turkey, Raki is a relative of Rakia. It pairs well with mezze or appetizers because of its strong anise taste.

Ouzo: Greece is home to ouzo, especially on the islands. This transparent liquor with an anise taste turns milky when combined with water. Enjoy a gentle sip while relishing the delicious seafood.

Pelinkovac

A herbal liqueur with a bitter taste that is popular in Serbia and Croatia. It is frequently used as an aperitif and is said to have digestive qualities.

Slivovitz

Slivovitz is a plum brandy with a fruity, spicy bite that is famous from Serbia. Locals may encourage you to try a batch they've produced themselves because they take great delight in doing so.

Every taste and mouthful conveys a fragment of the cultural fabric of the Balkans, adding to the uniqueness of your trip through this rich region.

CHAPTER 6

SHOPPING AND SOUVENIRS

Authentic Handicrafts and Artisanal Products

Traveling through the captivating Balkans will show you that this area is not just a shopping haven for people looking for genuine handicrafts and handcrafted goods, but also a treasure trove of breathtaking scenery and fascinating history.

Let's explore the world of Balkan shopping and the distinctive finds that are just waiting to be discovered.

1. Customized Crafts

The traditional crafts of the Balkans are richly varied, with distinct specializations found in each of the region's member nations. You will come across craftspeople who have refined their abilities over many generations, whether you are in Albania, Greece, Croatia, or any other country in the Balkans. Explore Bosnia and Herzegovina for its magnificent filigree jewelry, Croatia for its delicate lacework, and Bulgaria for its wonderfully woven fabrics. The passion and heart of the Balkans are captured in these handcrafted goods.

2. Pottery & Ceramics

The pottery from the Balkans are breathtaking. Local markets and boutique stores carry beautifully crafted, hand-painted earthenware. The region's varied culture and history are reflected in the colors and patterns. Balkan ceramics provide wonderful ornamental items as well as useful cookware

3. Embroidery and Textiles

Beautiful needlework from the Balkans is well-known, and it frequently narrates a tale of the regional way of life. Whether you use them on apparel, as accessories, or home décor, these intricate hand-stitched designs are a lovely way to bring a little bit of the Balkans into your home.

4. Jewels in Filigree

Particularly in Bosnia and Herzegovina, filigree jewelry is highly sought for. Fine strands of precious metals, such as gold and silver, are twisted and curled into delicate, lace-like designs in this complex craftsmanship. It's an exquisite illustration of Balkan artistry.

5. Symbolic Spirits

Raskia, or Balkan fruit brandies, are distinctive and delicious mementos even if they are not crafts in the conventional sense. There are several varieties available, each with a unique flavor. Drinks like cherry rakia in Serbia and quince rakia in Bulgaria provide a flavor of the hospitality seen across the Balkans.

Olive Oil & Regional Specialties

Balkan markets provide a wide selection of regional specialties for individuals who enjoy fine cuisine. Seek for premium olive oils in Greece and Croatia, or savor distinctive cheeses and fragrant spices throughout the area. The gourmet in you will find these items to be a delicious keepsake.

7. Conventional Clothing

Remember to check out the neighborhood businesses for clothes. The traditional clothing of the Balkans is richly varied, ranging from the vibrant sarafans in Bulgaria to the sophisticated in Greece. These things would be amazing presents or thoughtful additions to your own collection.

8. Regional Art

Balkan artists frequently find inspiration in the natural beauty and rich cultural legacy of the region. A vast variety of artwork is available, ranging from modern sculptures to paintings of landscapes. These items are a great way to add a little bit of the Balkan charm to your house as they perfectly represent the character of the area

Never Forget to Bargain

Haggling is a frequent practice at local marketplaces throughout several Balkan countries. Never be scared to haggle over costs as long as you do it politely. It might make for a pleasant and enlightening cultural experience while you shop.

Keep an eye out for these genuine handicrafts and handcrafted goods when you travel across the Balkans. They are not only exquisite keepsakes but also provide a window into the culture and history of this fascinating and varied area.

Local Markets and Bazaars

Visiting the regional markets and bazaars is one of the most enjoyable and engaging experiences you can have when visiting the Balkans. These dynamic, busy centers provide a singular glimpse into the customs, tastes, and culture of the area.

Here's a peek of what to anticipate when you venture into the heart of Balkan markets, from the vibrant kiosks of fresh food to artisan crafts.

1. Bosnia and Herzegovina, or Baščaršija, Sarajevo
Dating back to the fifteenth century, Sarajevo's ancient Baščaršija is a lively bazaar. Its cobblestone alleyways are lined with stores that provide handwoven fabrics, traditional Bosnian coffee sets, and elaborately made copperware. Remember to try cevapi, which is grilled minced beef, from a nearby food cart.

2. **North Macedonia's Skopje Old Bazaar**

The Old Bazaar in Skopje offers a quaint setting for shopping with its colorful blend of Byzantine and Ottoman buildings. Everything from jewelry and antiques to vibrant pottery may be found here. As you explore, don't forget to sample the local treats, such as baklava.

3. Turkey's Grand Bazaar in Istanbul

Despite not being in the Balkans, Istanbul's Grand Bazaar is famed and it's a must-visit for every tourist to the region. This winding bazaar, home to more than 4,000 stores, is a veritable gold mine of Turkish pleasures, ranging from spices and rugs to exquisitely patterned tiles and fabrics. Engage in bartering with store owners for a fully immersive encounter.

4. Croatia's Zadar Market

To explore the area's gastronomic gems, visit the busy market along the waterfront in Zadar. Fresh fish, cheeses, seasonal fruits and vegetables, and olive oils from the area are also abundant at the booths. It's a great location to experience Dalmatian cuisine.

5. The New Bazaar in Tirana, Albania

Tirana's New Bazaar is a chic location where the old and the new collide. You may purchase locally produced goods, organic goods, and crafts made in Albania here. Savor a cup of coffee at one of the charming cafés and take in the vibrant ambience.

6. The Kalenić Market in Belgrade, Serbia

Go to this vibrant market in the center of Belgrade to get fresh vegetables and regional specialties. It's a sensory extravaganza with smoked meats, specialty cheeses, and a wide variety of fruits and vegetables. For the liveliest experience, go there first thing in the morning.

7. North Macedonia's Ohrid Old Bazaar:

Ohrid's Old Bazaar is a charming location to purchase exquisite fabrics, vibrant ceramics, and handcrafted silver jewelry. It's a great area to pick up trinkets, and the winding pathways are rich in history.

8. Regional Specialties

Local dishes may also be enjoyed at Balkan marketplaces. Don't pass up the chance to sample freshly made bread and pastries, as well as Balkan street cuisine like baklava, ajvar, and burek, which are savory pastries.

It's not only about buying when you visit the Balkans' local markets and bazaars it's also about fully experiencing the diverse range of customs, cuisines, and cultures that make up the area. Thus, be sure to schedule some time to explore these lively marketplaces, engage with the people, and savor the distinctive experiences they have to offer when you're in the Balkans.

Unique Souvenirs Reflecting Balkan Culture

You will come across a world of rich and varied civilizations along the way, each with its own history, customs, and tales to tell, when you travel across the Balkans. Taking home one-of-a-kind mementos that capture the spirit of your Balkan experience is one of the greatest ways to do it.
These items should represent the region's colorful tapestry.

Here's a list of some amazing mementos you may gather to treasure your Balkan experiences, from Croatia to Greece and all the nations in between.

Turkey's centuries-old heritage of exquisite carpet making is reflected in its hand woven carpets and rugs. These carpets are artworks that narrate tales of Turkish history, not merely decorative pieces for the house. Regardless of the size of the carpet or rug you select, it's a piece of history you can bring back to your house.

Greek Olive Oil

Greece is known for producing excellent olive oil. In addition to being a delectable memento, a bottle of extra-virgin olive oil from a nearby olive field offers a sense of Mediterranean culture.

Traditional Rose Oil from Bulgaria

The breathtaking rose fields in Bulgaria are the source of the nation's renowned rose oil. This priceless and aromatic oil is utilized in cosmetics, fragrances, and even food recipes.

Matryoshka Dolls (Serbia)

Although most people connect matryoshka dolls with Russia, they are also available in Serbia, frequently with a distinctive Balkan twist. These beautiful keepsakes are hand-painted dolls that nest together and feature local characteristics.

Handmade Jewelry (Croatia)

The country is home to gifted jewelers who produce one-of-a-kind items that draw inspiration from the Mediterranean and Adriatic Sea. Seek for products with vivid blue hues, which are frequently associated with the water.

Traditional Musical Instruments of the Balkans (Macedonia)

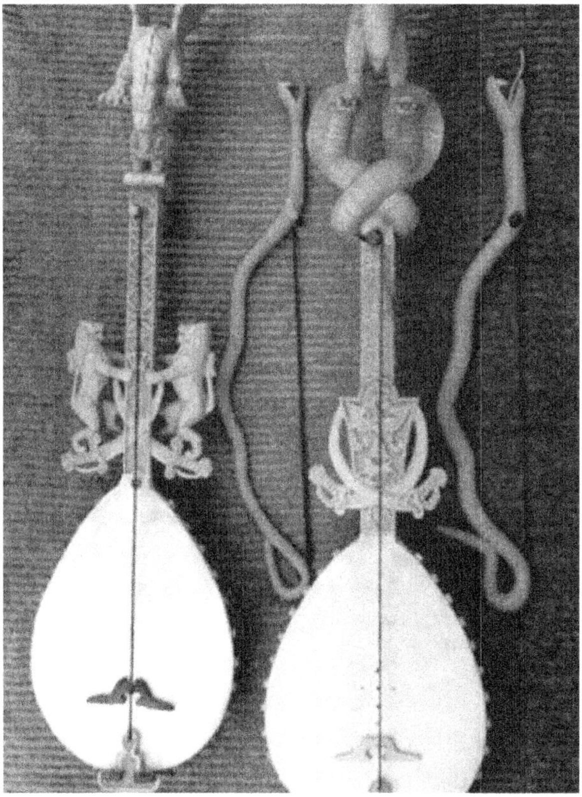

Music lovers can purchase a range of traditional musical instruments from the Žurla to the Gajda, which are genuine and distinctive keepsakes.

Bosnia and Herzegovina Hand-Painted Ceramics

The artists in this region are renowned for their exquisitely painted ceramics. Vases, bowls, and plates with elaborate designs and vivid colors are available.

Croatian Lavender goods: The aromatic lavender goods, such as soaps, sachets, and essential oils, are produced from the country's stunning lavender fields on the island of Hvar.

Albanian traditional kilims

Kilims are woven carpets that are representative of Albanian culture. They have distinctive patterns and colors. They work well as tablecloths, wall hangings, and carpets.

Copperware (Montenegro)

The region is well-known for its copperware, which includes beautifully crafted coffee pots and ornamental pieces that showcase the artisanal workmanship of the area.

Handcrafted Rakia (Various Balkan Countries): Throughout the Balkans, rakia is a well-liked fruit brandy. You may practically get a taste of the spirit of every Balkan country by bringing home a bottle of the locally made rakia.

These are only a handful of the many interesting and varied mementos that may be found all around the Balkans. Although every nation has its own specialties, they are all united by a warm welcome and a diverse range of cultural experiences.

Therefore, when you're seeing the Balkans' quaint towns, lively marketplaces, and ancient cities, don't forget to bring home a little bit of this alluring country. In addition to enhancing your living area, your mementos will serve as a constant reminder of the amazing adventure you took deep within the Balkans.

CHAPTER 7

ACCOMMODATION OPTIONS

Luxurious Hotels and Resorts

Visitors visiting the Balkans are in for a treat when it comes to opulent lodging. Rich in history and breathtaking scenery, this varied area has a variety of luxurious hotels and resorts to suit the needs of those looking for a decadent getaway.

There are luxurious alternatives available for an opulent stay, whether you're lounging on the Adriatic shore or seeing the old cities.

1. Montenegro's Aman Sveti Stefan

World-famous Aman Sveti Stefan resort is situated on a private island on the Adriatic coast. This upscale location blends contemporary style with a fishing town from the fifteenth century. Luxurious lodging, exclusive beaches, and superb dining are available to visitors. An idyllic scene is created by the views of the glistening sea and the quaint settlement.

2. Slovenia's Kempinski Palace Portorož

A real jewel on the Adriatic is the Kempinski Palace Portorož in Slovenia. With its Belle Époque architecture, this opulent hotel gives visitors a window into a more opulent time in history. The hotel has an amazing spa, beautiful views of the sea, and excellent service. It's the ideal option for anyone looking for a peaceful getaway with a hint of nostalgia.

3. Greece's Porto Carras Grand Resort

Situated on the stunning peninsula of Halkidiki, the Porto Carras Grand Resort is an expansive sanctuary of opulence. This resort offers a comprehensive experience with its own marina, golf course, and many dining options. It's the perfect place for a laid-back Mediterranean vacation because of the beautiful gardens and tranquil beaches.

4. Montenegro's Chedi Lustica Bay

Situated on the breathtaking Montenegrin shore, the Chedi Lustica Bay is a sophisticated and contemporary resort. Travelers seeking refinement are drawn to it by its ultramodern design and first-rate amenities. It's a great pick for luxury seekers because of the views of the marina, the private beach, and the beautiful bay.

5. Sarajevo, Bosnia and Herzegovina; Hotel Europe

The Hotel Europe is a historical symbol of grandeur located in the center of Sarajevo. This hotel from the 19th century blends classic style with contemporary amenities. Because of its convenient location, visitors may spend their days exploring the rich cultural and historical offerings of the city and finish their days in an opulent hideaway.

6. Estonia's Hotel Telegraaf

The Hotel Telegraaf in Tallinn, Estonia, is an opulent option for those who are interested in seeing the Balkans in northern Europe. It combines history and luxury in a telegraph building from the 19th century. The hotel's upscale restaurant and spa provide an opulent experience amid Tallinn's quaint Old Town.

Luxurious hotels and resorts in the Balkans provide visitors with the chance to take in the breathtaking scenery and diverse cultural offerings in addition to providing opulent lodging. There are plenty of sophisticated alternatives to make your trip to the Balkans genuinely unforgettable, whether you're experiencing the ancient capitals of Bosnia and Herzegovina, the stunning beaches of Montenegro, or the charming alleyways of Tallinn.

Charming Bed and Breakfasts

Amidst the breathtaking natural landscapes and storied past of the Balkans, you'll uncover an abundance of delightful bed and breakfasts that don't merely offer a place to lay your head but promise a truly distinctive and genuine travel experience. Whether you're enticed by the awe-inspiring mountain panoramas, the postcard-perfect coastal towns, or the historically-rich cities, there's a welcoming B&B eager to embrace your arrival.

Let's set out on a journey through some of the region's most captivating B&Bs:

Magnificent Views in Montenegro:
Location: Kotor, Montenegro
What Makes it Special: Picture waking up to the awe-inspiring sight of the Bay of Kotor, a UNESCO World Heritage site. These B&Bs seamlessly blend historic charm with contemporary comfort, all while the grand city walls stand as your immediate neighbors.

Tranquil Countryside in Romania
Location: Transylvania, Romania
What Makes it Special: In the heart of Transylvania, you'll stumble upon B&Bs nestled in serene countryside, encircled by the legendary Carpathian Mountains. Experience the warm hospitality of local hosts and embark on journeys to Dracula's Castle and quaint villages.

Seaside Serenity in Croatia
Location: Dalmatian Coast, Croatia
What Makes it Special: Uncover B&Bs along the dazzling Dalmatian Coast, where these charming retreats offer convenient access to crystal-clear waters, historic towns, and mouthwatering Mediterranean cuisine.

Historical Hideaways in Bosnia and Herzegovina:
Location: Mostar, Bosnia and Herzegovina
What Makes it Special: Immerse yourself in the rich history of Mostar, renowned for its iconic bridge. Choose to stay in charming B&Bs that overlook the Neretva River, allowing you to savor the city's vibrant ambiance.

Majestic Mountains in Bulgaria
Location: Bansko, Bulgaria
What Makes it Special: For those passionate about winter sports, Bansko offers snug B&Bs that serve as the perfect launchpad for skiing and snowboarding in the Pirin Mountains. In the summer, this region transforms into a haven for hikers.

City Charms in Serbia
Location: Belgrade, Serbia
What Makes it Special: Belgrade's B&Bs are ideally situated in the heart of the bustling city. Here, you can explore the vivacious nightlife, iconic landmarks, and the warm-hearted welcome of the Serbian people.

Idyllic Retreats in Slovenia
Location: Lake Bled, Slovenia
What Makes it Special: Lake Bled's B&Bs offer a peaceful escape amid the Julian Alps. You can stay in cozy accommodations that overlook the emerald lake and pay a visit to the renowned Bled Castle.

Coastal Allure in Greece
Location: Santorini, Greece (Yes, we're crossing borders!)
What Makes it Special: The picturesque island of Santorini boasts B&Bs that provide panoramic vistas of the Aegean Sea and the famous caldera. These accommodations allow you to soak in the sun and savor the island's distinct charm.

B&Bs in the Balkans transcend mere lodging; they act as gateways to genuine experiences, warm hospitality, and the rich cultural tapestry that this diverse region offers. No matter which corner of the Balkans captures your heart, you'll find inviting B&Bs ready to transform your journey into an unforgettable adventure. So, pack your bags and embark on a voyage filled with stunning landscapes and heartfelt moments in these snug retreats.

Budget-Friendly Hostels and Guesthouses

When embarking on a budget-friendly exploration of the Balkans, the quest for economical yet comfortable lodging becomes a top priority. Fortunately, this region boasts a diverse selection of cost-effective hostels and guesthouses that not only contribute to your financial savings but also immerse you in the local culture.

Here, we present a guide to some exceptional choices:

Sarajevo, Bosnia and Herzegovina
The Doctor's House – This charming hostel, nestled in the heart of Sarajevo, not only boasts affordability but is also renowned for its welcoming ambiance. Here, you can relish a homemade breakfast while mingling with fellow travelers.

Skopje, North Macedonia
Shanti Hostel – A lively and reasonably priced hostel that provides comfortable dormitories and private rooms. It serves as an excellent hub for meeting other travelers and relishing the city's nightlife.

Budva, Montenegro
Freedom Hostel – This gem of budget-friendly accommodation is conveniently located within walking distance of the picturesque Budva Old Town and the pristine beach. The hospitable staff ensures your stay is memorable.
Thessaloniki, Greece:

Little Big House , Nestled in a historic edifice, this stylish hostel offers dorms and private rooms with a distinctive bohemian allure. It's conveniently situated a short stroll from the city center, making it an ideal base for exploring Thessaloniki.

Belgrade, Serbia:

Hedonist Hostel – Found in the vibrant Savamala district, this hostel is celebrated for its sociable atmosphere. The staff frequently organize events and tours, making it effortless to connect with fellow travelers.

Dubrovnik, Croatia

Hostel Angelina – Operated by a welcoming family, this hostel is a brief bus ride away from the Old Town, offering a peaceful and economical escape from the tourist crowds.

Tirana, Albania:

Trip'n Hostel – A relaxed hostel featuring a bar and a friendly ambiance, making it an ideal starting point for your exploration of Albania's capital.

Ohrid, North Macedonia

Sunny Lake Hostel – Positioned in proximity to the breathtaking Lake Ohrid, this budget-friendly hostel provides rooms with scenic lake views and a delightful garden, creating a serene retreat for budget-conscious travelers.

Mostar, Bosnia and Herzegovina

Majdas Touch Hostel – Managed by the hospitable Majda, this hostel is renowned for its homely atmosphere. Majda arranges tours and dinners, ensuring you get the best of the Mostar experience.

Sofia, Bulgaria

Hostel Mostel – This hostel offers remarkable value, including complimentary dinners, a convivial atmosphere, and a prime location in Sofia's city center.

These economical hostels and guesthouses in the Balkans not only help you manage your expenses but also enrich your journey with unforgettable experiences. Many of these establishments go beyond the basics of providing a place to sleep; they foster a sense of community and offer valuable local insights, leaving you with cherished memories of your travels in this captivating and diverse region.

CHAPTER 8

PRACTICAL INFORMATION AND TIP

7 days Itinerary

If you're gearing up for an adventure in the captivating Balkans, be prepared to immerse yourself in a vibrant blend of history, culture, and the breathtaking beauty of the region.

Below is a 7-day travel plan designed to help you get the most out of your exploration:

Day 1: Commence your journey in Zagreb, Croatia. This city, the capital of Croatia, beckons with its rich history and charm. Take time to discover the historic Upper Town, visit the iconic St. Mark's Church, and meander through the picturesque streets. Cap off your day with a delectable taste of traditional Croatian cuisine for dinner.

Day 2: Depart for Ljubljana, the delightful capital of Slovenia. In this enchanting city, stroll through the old town, savor a leisurely walk along the Ljubljanica River, and ascend Ljubljana Castle for panoramic vistas. Wind down your evening in one of the cozy cafes.

Day 3: Embark on a day trip to the stunning Lake Bled and Lake Bohinj, both ensconced in the Julian Alps. Tour Bled Castle, traverse the tranquil waters to Bled Island on a traditional boat, and bask in the astounding natural splendor of Bohinj.

Day 4: Traverse southward to Croatia's Plitvice Lakes National Park, where you can spend the day navigating wooden walkways and admiring the mesmerizing waterfalls set amidst lush green landscapes.

Day 5: Venture to the coastal town of Zadar, Croatia. Explore the historic old town, where Roman ruins are interwoven with the enchanting melodies of the Sea Organ. As the day draws to a close, be sure to witness the breathtaking sunset by the iconic Greeting to the Sun installation.

Day 6: Continue your journey south to Split, Croatia, where you'll dive into the history enshrined in Diocletian's Palace, a UNESCO World Heritage Site. Roam the bustling Old Town, pay a visit to the Cathedral of St. Domnius, and savor a delightful seafood feast at a local eatery.

Day 7: Conclude your remarkable expedition in Dubrovnik, often referred to as the Pearl of the Adriatic. Walk along the city walls, explore historical sites, and relish the awe-inspiring vistas of the Adriatic Sea. Don't miss the opportunity to savor the local cuisine and unwind by the coast.

Additional Suggestions

Consider adding a day trip to Mostar, Bosnia and Herzegovina, to witness the iconic Stari Most bridge.

If you have more time at your disposal, contemplate an exploration of the Montenegro coast or the Greek islands within the Balkans.

Keep in mind that travel durations between destinations may vary, so plan your itinerary thoughtfully.

This 7-day adventure through the Balkans offers a tantalizing glimpse into the region's history, culture, and natural beauty. Make sure to relish the local flavors and soak up the unique ambiance of each destination.

Money matters in Balkans

The situation is the same when it comes to currencies. Various nations in the Balkans have their own monetary units, but the Euro (EUR) is widely recognized in specific regions, especially in popular tourist areas.
Here's a brief overview of some of the primary currencies:

Euro (EUR): Employed in countries such as Montenegro and Kosovo.

Serbian Dinar (RSD): The official currency of Serbia.

Croatian Kuna (HRK): Utilized in Croatia.
Bulgarian Lev (BGN): The currency of Bulgaria.

Bosnian Convertible Mark (BAM): In use in Bosnia and Herzegovina.

Albanian Lek (ALL): The official currency in Albania.

Currency Exchange and ATMs
Currency exchange bureaus are readily available in major cities and tourist hotspots, simplifying the process of converting your money.
However, it's advisable to exercise caution regarding exchange rates and associated fees, which can vary between locations. Typically, for more favorable rates, it is wise to perform currency exchanges at banks rather than at airport kiosks.

ATMs are prevalent in most Balkan countries and are generally the most convenient means of acquiring local currency. Nevertheless, it's prudent to consult your bank regarding potential international withdrawal fees. Some ATMs may offer to process transactions in your home currency, but opting for the local currency usually yields a more advantageous exchange rate.

Credit Cards and Payments

Credit and debit cards are widely accepted in urban centers and tourist hubs. Yet, in remote or rural areas, cash remains the preferred form of payment. It's a judicious idea to have some local currency on hand.

Visa and Mastercard are commonly recognized, while American Express and Discover cards may not enjoy the same level of recognition. Notifying your bank of your travel plans can help prevent issues with card usage abroad.

Budgeting and Expenses

The Balkans are celebrated for their budget-friendly appeal, offering economical options for accommodations, dining, and transportation. Costs can vary depending on your location, with certain areas, like Croatia, being more costly than others.

To efficiently manage your expenses

Conduct research on average expenses in the specific Balkan countries you intend to explore.

Consider savoring local cuisine at budget-friendly eateries and cafes.

Opt for cost-effective transportation options, such as public transit or car rentals.
Seek out budget-friendly lodgings, including guesthouses, hostels, or apartments.

Tipping Customs
Tipping practices may differ from one Balkan country to another. In certain places, such as Croatia, leaving a gratuity is customary, while in others, like Serbia, it may not be as common. As a general guideline, rounding up the bill or leaving a 10% tip is often appreciated.

A thorough grasp of the financial landscape in the Balkans is crucial for a seamless and enjoyable travel adventure. By adopting the right strategies concerning currency, payments, and financial planning, you can make the most of your journey through this diverse and enthralling region while maintaining control over your monetary affairs. May your Balkans journey be filled with wonderful experiences!

Safety Guidelines for Travelers

Traveling through the Balkans offers an exciting and culturally immersive experience. However, just like any other travel destination, it's crucial to prioritize safety throughout your journey. Here, we provide practical safety recommendations for travelers in the Balkans:

Conduct In-Depth Research about Your Destination
Commence your travel preparations by delving into the specifics of the countries you intend to visit. This includes

understanding local customs, legal regulations, and potential safety considerations. Each Balkan nation boasts its distinct characteristics and nuances.

Stay Well-Informed

Stay up-to-date with the latest travel advisories from your government's official website. This invaluable resource offers essential insights into safety concerns and the political climate within the Balkan countries on your itinerary.

Be Wary of Local Currency and Scams

Exercise caution when it comes to currency exchange. Opt for official exchange offices or reliable ATMs. Stay vigilant against currency exchange scams and unlicensed street vendors.

Prioritize Transportation Safety

Opt for reputable transportation services. Ensure that taxis are licensed, and if they don't use a meter, negotiate fares upfront. In major cities, public transportation is typically safe and dependable.

Guard Against Petty Theft

Just like many other tourist destinations, petty theft can be a concern. Keep a watchful eye on your possessions, particularly in crowded areas and tourist hotspots. Consider using anti-theft bags or pouches for safeguarding your valuables.

Familiarize Yourself with Emergency Numbers

Acquaint yourself with the local emergency contact numbers in each country you plan to explore. These numbers may vary, so it's essential to be well-informed about the specific ones applicable to your destination.

Prioritize Health Precautions

Ensure that your vaccinations are up to date and carry any necessary medications. Opt for bottled water and exercise caution when consuming street food in areas with questionable hygiene practices.

Overcome Language Barriers

While English isn't universally spoken in the Balkans, learning a few basic phrases in the local language can prove immensely beneficial in unforeseen circumstances.

Respect Local Customs

The Balkans boast a rich tapestry of cultures and traditions, and it's important to show respect for local customs. Exercise mindfulness regarding dress codes and etiquette when visiting religious sites, and always seek permission before photographing people.

Secure Comprehensive Travel Insurance

It's a prudent decision to secure comprehensive travel insurance that covers medical emergencies, trip cancellations, and theft. Ensure you have a firm grasp of the terms and conditions of your policy.

Prioritize Safety in Natural Environments

If you plan to explore the stunning natural landscapes of the Balkans, such as national parks and hiking trails, be well-prepared with the appropriate gear and maps. Always inform someone about your plans, and consider hiring a local guide for remote areas.

Considerations for LGBTQ+ Travelers

While societal attitudes are evolving, some Balkan countries may not be as LGBTQ+ friendly as others. It's advisable to research the local LGBTQ+ scene and exercise caution with public displays of affection.

Trust Your Instincts

Your instincts often serve as your most reliable guide. If a situation feels unsafe, it's better to err on the side of caution.

Maintain Connectivity

Keep your loved ones informed about your whereabouts and travel plans. Share your itinerary and contact details with someone you trust.

Traveling through the Balkans can be a gratifying adventure. By heeding these safety guidelines and remaining vigilant of your surroundings, you can maximize your journey while ensuring a secure and enjoyable experience in this diverse and historically rich region.

Language Basics and Useful Phrases

When embarking on your journey through the Balkans, having a grasp of the local language can significantly enhance your experience and foster meaningful connections with the residents. Below, we offer a concise introduction to language essentials and a selection of practical phrases to assist you:

Key Language Concepts in the Balkans

The Balkan region boasts a rich tapestry of languages. While English is often spoken in tourist hubs, demonstrating an effort to communicate in the local tongue is met with appreciation.

The Balkans encompass various languages, including:

Croatian: Spoken in Croatia and portions of Bosnia and Herzegovina.

Serbian: Found in Serbia, Montenegro, and parts of Bosnia and Herzegovina.

Bosnian: Also spoken in Bosnia and Herzegovina.

Albanian: The official language in Albania and widely used in Kosovo and sections of North Macedonia.

Greek: The primary language in Greece.

Bulgarian: Spoken in Bulgaria and areas of North Macedonia.

Romanian: The official language of Romania and Moldova.

Practical Phrases

Greetings
Croatian/Serbian/Bosnian: "Zdravo" (Здраво)

Albanian: "Përshëndetje"

Greek: "Γειά σας" (Yia sas)

Bulgarian: "Здравей" (Zdravey)

Romanian: "Salut"

Politeness:
Croatian/Serbian/Bosnian: "Molim" (Молим)

Albanian: "Ju lutem"

Greek: "Παρακαλώ" (Parakaló)

Bulgarian: "Моля" (Molya)

Romanian: "Te rog"

Expressing Gratitude
Croatian/Serbian/Bosnian: "Hvala" (Хвала)

Albanian: "Faleminderit"

Greek: "Ευχαριστώ" (Efcharistó)

Bulgarian: "Благодаря" (Blagodarya)

Romanian: "Mulțumesc"

Affirmation
Croatian/Serbian/Bosnian: "Da" (Да)

Albanian: "Po"

Greek: "Ναι" (Ne)

Bulgarian: "Да" (Da)

Romanian: "Da"

Negation
Croatian/Serbian/Bosnian: "Ne" (Не)

Albanian: "Jo"

Greek: "Όχι" (Óchi)

Bulgarian: "Не" (Ne)

Romanian: "Nu"

Apologies and Requests
Croatian/Serbian/Bosnian:"Izvinite" (Извините)

Albanian: "Më falni"

Greek: "Συγγνώμη" (Signómi)

Bulgarian: "Извинете" (Izvinete)

Romanian: "Scuzați-mă"

Seeking Directions
Croatian/Serbian/Bosnian: "Gdje je...?" (Где je...?)

Albanian: "Ku është...?"

Greek: "Πού είναι...;" (Pou íne...?)

Bulgarian: "Къде е...?" (Kŭde e...?)

Romanian: "Unde este...?"

Pricing Inquiries
Croatian/Serbian/Bosnian: "Koliko košta ovo?"

Albanian: "Sa kushton kjo?"

Greek: "Πόσο κοστίζει αυτό;"

Bulgarian: "Колко струва това?"

Romanian: "Cât costă acesta?"

Requests for Assistance:
Croatian/Serbian/Bosnian: "Treba mi pomoć" (Треба ми помоћ)

Albanian: "Më duhet ndihmë"

Greek: "Χρειάζομαι βοήθεια" (Chreiázomai voítheia)

Bulgarian: "Нуждая се от помощ" (Nuzhdaya se ot pomosht)

Romanian: "Am nevoie de ajutor"

Farewells
Croatian/Serbian/Bosnian:"Doviđenja" (Довиђења)

Albanian: "Mirupafshim"

Greek: "Αντίο" (Antío)

Bulgarian: "Довиждане" (Dovizhdane)

Romanian: "La revedere"

As you set out on your Balkan adventure, remember that even a modest effort to speak the local language, whether it's a warm greeting or a heartfelt thank you, can make a positive impact and help you navigate more smoothly. Most locals appreciate the gesture and view it as a sign of respect and cultural curiosity.

Emergency Contacts and Medical Services

Exploring the enchanting Balkans offers an exhilarating experience, yet it is crucial to stay prepared for unforeseen circumstances. Below is a practical guide to emergency contacts and healthcare services in the Balkans, ensuring that your travels remain not only unforgettable but also secure:

Emergency Contacts

General Emergencies: In most Balkan countries, dial 112 to access emergency services, including the police, fire department, and medical assistance. Always ensure that your phone is charged and easily accessible.

Police Services: For non-urgent situations or to report a crime, contact the local police by dialing 192.

Medical Emergencies: In the event of an immediate medical crisis, call 194. For less pressing health concerns, you can seek assistance at local hospitals or clinics (more details below).

Fire Department: If you encounter a fire-related emergency, dial 193 to reach the fire department.

Mountain Rescue: When exploring the Balkan mountains, rest assured that mountain rescue services are available. The specific contact number may vary by country, so it's advisable to inquire locally.

Medical Services

Hospitals and Clinics: Major Balkan cities such as Belgrade, Zagreb, Sofia, and Bucharest are equipped with modern medical facilities. English-speaking staff is typically available in these urban centers.

Health Insurance: Before embarking on your Balkans journey, it's imperative to have comprehensive travel insurance that covers medical emergencies. Many hospitals may require upfront payments, which can be later reimbursed through your insurance provider.

Pharmacies: Pharmacies are prevalent in nearly every town across the Balkans. Look for the recognizable green cross sign, denoting a pharmacy. Pharmacists can provide guidance on over-the-counter remedies and frequently speak English.

Vaccinations and Health Precautions: Depending on your chosen destination within the Balkans, it's advisable to ascertain if specific vaccinations or health precautions are recommended before your trip.

Medical Translators: If your journey takes you to more remote areas where English might not be widely understood, consider carrying a medical translation app or a small phrasebook to assist in communicating your health needs.

Traveler's Tips

Emergency Kit: Carry a basic first-aid kit containing essentials like bandages, pain relievers, antiseptic wipes, and any prescribed medications.

Emergency Contacts: Save the local emergency numbers and the contact details of your country's embassy or consulate in your phone.

Travel Companions: If you're traveling with others, ensure they are informed about your medical conditions and any allergies you may have.

Allergies and Dietary Restrictions: If you have food allergies or specific dietary requirements, familiarize yourself with how to communicate these in the local language to prevent cross-contamination or misunderstandings.

Travel Insurance: Emphasizing the significance of comprehensive travel insurance. It can be a lifeline in the event of an emergency.

Always remember that your safety and well-being are paramount when navigating the diverse and captivating Balkans. With a bit of preparation and knowledge, you can embark on your journey with confidence and peace of mind.

CONCLUSION

Embarking on a journey through the enchanting Balkans is a voyage that goes beyond the ordinary, immersing you in a rich tapestry of history, culture, and natural splendor. Within the pages of this travel guide, we've ventured through the varied and captivating landscapes of the Balkan Peninsula, offering valuable insights and recommendations to ensure your journey is truly unforgettable. As we bring our exploration to a close, let's take a moment to reflect on the key takeaways and parting thoughts.

Diversity within Unity

The Balkans present a paradoxical blend of diversity and unity. Encompassing countries like Croatia, Serbia, Bulgaria, Greece, Albania, and more, this region is a mosaic of cultures, languages, and traditions. However, it's bound together by a shared history and a heartwarming sense of hospitality. Our conclusion here is that it's this fusion of the old and the new, the juxtaposition of landscapes, and the diverse culinary offerings that render the Balkans an irresistible destination.

Historical Echoes

The Balkans have stood as a crossroads of civilizations for countless centuries, leaving behind layers of history etched in both stone and spirit. From the ancient ruins of Rome and Byzantine frescoes to the opulent palaces of the Ottoman

Empire and the remnants of the communist era, the past is ever-present in these lands.
As travelers, we are compelled to conclude that truly comprehending the Balkans necessitates embracing this rich tapestry of historical narratives.

Nature's Grandeur

The Balkan landscapes are a revelation to the senses. Pristine beaches lining the Adriatic, the awe-inspiring cliffs of Montenegro's Bay of Kotor, the majestic peaks of the Dinaric Alps, and the tranquil meandering of the Danube River through Hungary and Croatia represent just a small sample.
Our conclusion here is that those with a penchant for nature and a spirit of adventure will discover both solace and exhilaration amidst these breathtaking vistas.

Culinary Treasures

Balkan cuisine is a delightful amalgamation of flavors. From the seafood-rich coastal dishes to the hearty stews and grilled specialties of the interior, every meal is an open invitation to explore the tastes of the region. The conclusion is uncomplicated – be prepared to pamper your taste buds with fresh ingredients and delectable dishes, and make sure not to depart without sampling the regional wines and rakija (fruit brandy).

Heartfelt Encounters

Interacting with the people of the Balkans is an enriching journey in itself. The locals are known for their warmth, welcoming spirit, and deep pride in their heritage. Engage in conversations, learn a few local phrases, and you'll uncover the very heart and soul of these lands. The conclusion is that it's these personal interactions that create enduring memories and a profound understanding of the region.

Practical Insights for Travel

Throughout this guide, we've offered practical travel tips and insights to assist you in planning your Balkan adventure. Whether it's guidance on visa requirements, transportation options, cultural etiquette, or safety precautions, the conclusion is evident – meticulous planning and preparation can significantly enhance the smoothness and enjoyment of your journey.

Exploring the Balkans is a journey through the familiar and the unknown. It's an odyssey where ancient cities harmonize with modern metropolises, where awe-inspiring landscapes coexist with tranquil countryside, and where diverse cultures flourish in harmony. As you traverse this captivating region, we trust that you'll arrive at the conclusion that the Balkans are a trove of remarkable experiences awaiting your discovery. So, pack your bags, embrace the adventure, and embark on an exploration of this enigmatic corner of Europe - the Balkans.

Further Resources

Recommended Reading on the Balkans
Here is a selection of recommended readings for those who wish to explore the Balkans in greater depth, gaining insights into its history, culture, and travel experiences in this captivating region.

"Balkan Ghosts: A Journey Through History" by Robert D. Kaplan
This renowned book embarks on a captivating journey through the Balkans, offering a historical and geopolitical perspective on the region's intricate and often tumultuous past. Kaplan's vivid narrative brings the Balkans' history to life.

"Black Lamb and Grey Falcon" by Rebecca West
Rebecca West's opus provides a sweeping account of her travels in Yugoslavia during the 1930s. It weaves together a rich tapestry of history, culture, and personal anecdotes, offering profound insights into the region.

"The Balkans: Nationalism, War, and the Great Powers, 1804-1999" by Misha Glenny
For a comprehensive grasp of the modern history of the Balkans, this book is an excellent choice. It delves into the intricate interplay between nationalism, international politics, and the series of conflicts that have shaped the Balkans.

"The Balkans: A Short History" by Mark Mazower
Mark Mazower offers a concise yet informative overview of Balkans history, tracing its evolution from ancient times to the present day. It serves as a superb starting point for those seeking to understand the pivotal historical events.

"The Bridge on the Drina" by Ivo Andrić
A Nobel Prize-winning novel by Yugoslav author Ivo Andrić, this work is essential for anyone interested in the Balkans. It explores the region's history and culture through the narrative of a bridge in the town of Višegrad.

"The Balkans: Minorities and States in Conflict" edited by Hugh Poulton
This compilation of essays offers valuable insights into the ethnic and political conflicts that have characterized the Balkans in the 20th century. It provides context for comprehending the intricacies of the region's recent history.

"Balkans, 1804-2012: Nationalism, War and the Great Powers" by Brendan Simms
An exploration of the modern Balkans, this book examines the region's history through the lenses of nationalism and the involvement of great powers. It's an invaluable resource for understanding the contemporary dynamics of the Balkans.

"The Balkans: A Post-Communist History" by Robert Bideleux and Ian Jeffries
Focusing on the post-communist era, this book presents a detailed account of the Balkans' transformation since the fall

of the Iron Curtain. It covers political, economic, and social changes in the region.

"Lonely Planet Western Balkans" by Lonely Planet
If you're planning to explore the Balkans, this travel guide by Lonely Planet is an exceptional resource. It offers comprehensive information on various Balkan countries, including travel tips, accommodation recommendations, and cultural insights.

These books provide a diverse array of perspectives on the Balkans, ranging from historical accounts to contemporary analyses, and travel guides to prepare you for your adventure. They will enrich your understanding of this captivating region, whether you're an armchair traveler or planning to visit the Balkans in person."

Online Travel Tools and Apps

Enhance your travel experience with the help of online travel tools and apps. Here's a selection of top resources to make your exploration of this vibrant region even more enjoyable:

1. **Google Maps**
Whether you're strolling through Dubrovnik's charming cobblestone streets, hiking in the breathtaking Plitvice Lakes National Park, or navigating the bustling thoroughfares of Belgrade, Google Maps is your reliable companion. It provides real-time directions, user reviews, and photos, ensuring you explore with confidence.

2. Skyscanner
Finding the best flight deals to the Balkans is a breeze with Skyscanner. This app compares flights from multiple airlines and travel agencies, guaranteeing you access to the most budget-friendly tickets for your journey.

3**. TripAdvisor**
Are you eager to uncover the top-rated restaurants in Sarajevo or discover hidden gems in Sofia? TripAdvisor is your go-to source for user-generated reviews and recommendations for hotels, eateries, and attractions across the Balkans.

4. Couchsurfing

For a distinctive and budget-friendly travel experience, consider Couchsurfing. This platform connects travelers with locals who offer complimentary accommodations, cultural insights, and even guided tours in cities throughout the Balkans.

5. XE Currency Converter

While meandering through various Balkan countries, it's essential to stay informed about currency exchange rates. XE Currency Converter allows you to effortlessly convert currencies on the go, ensuring you get the most value for your money.

6. Duolingo

Connecting with locals is a gratifying aspect of travel. Duolingo provides free language courses, including Serbo-Croatian, Bulgarian, and other Balkan languages, facilitating communication with the people you meet on your journey.

7. Booking.com

Secure comfortable accommodations in the Balkans with Booking.com. This platform offers a diverse array of options, from luxurious hotels in Dubrovnik to cozy guesthouses in Skopje.

8. Yelp

When you're in search of the finest local dining experiences, Yelp is your ultimate app. It provides reviews and ratings for restaurants and cafes in various Balkan cities, ensuring you savor the culinary delights of the region.

9. Google Translate
Overcoming language barriers can be challenging, but Google Translate is your ally. It allows you to translate text and even engage in conversations in different languages, making communication smoother.

10. Weather.com
The Balkans' climate can vary significantly, so staying updated on the weather is vital. Weather.com delivers up-to-the-minute forecasts for cities across the region, ensuring you're well-prepared for whatever nature has in store.

Make the most of your journey through the Balkans by embracing its beauty and diversity. Utilize these online travel tools and apps to ensure a seamless and enjoyable travel experience. With these valuable resources at your fingertips, you'll be fully prepared to explore and savor all that this captivating region has to offer.

Tips for Solo Travelers and Families

Exploring the Balkans can be a delightful experience for both individual travelers and families alike. This region is brimming with a rich tapestry of history, culture, and breathtaking natural landscapes. Below, you'll find valuable advice to maximize your Balkans escapade, whether you're embarking on a solitary adventure or venturing with your loved ones.

For Solo Travelers

Prioritize Safety: While the Balkans are generally safe, exercising common-sense precautions is wise. Stay vigilant in unfamiliar locales, safeguard your belongings, and inform someone back home about your travel plans.

Learn the Basics: Familiarize yourself with a few local phrases as it can greatly enhance your interactions. The effort is appreciated by locals and can make your experiences more enjoyable.

Connect with Locals: Make an effort to engage with local residents. This can lead to enriching encounters and provide valuable insights into the region's culture and history.

Consider Hostels: Hostels are excellent places to meet fellow travelers, forge new friendships, and keep to a budget. Many also offer organized group activities.

Utilize Public Transport: The Balkans boast an extensive and cost-effective public transportation network. Trains and buses are fantastic options for exploring the region and meeting locals along the way.

Embrace New Cuisines: Balkan cuisine is diverse and delectable. Don't hesitate to savor local dishes, and street food can be both budget-friendly and flavorful.

Solo Adventures: Explore off-the-beaten-path destinations and embark on hikes through the stunning national parks. The Balkans offer numerous opportunities for solo adventurers to immerse themselves in nature.

For Families

Select Family-Friendly Activities: The Balkans offer a variety of family-oriented activities. Seek out museums, parks, and cultural events that cater to children's interests.

Pack Essentials: Ensure you have all the necessary items for your children, from travel-friendly snacks to any required medications. Packing light is convenient, but don't overlook the essentials.

Accommodations: Opt for family-friendly lodging options. Many hotels and guesthouses provide amenities such as cribs and high chairs. Booking accommodations with a kitchen can make meal preparation for kids more convenient.

Take It Slow: The Balkans are culturally diverse, so consider breaking your journey into smaller segments. Gradually travel between cities or regions to minimize stress on your children.

Encourage Cultural Learning: Leverage this opportunity to introduce your kids to various cultures and histories. Explore historical sites and partake in local traditions, making the learning experience enjoyable.

Prioritize Health: Ensure your family's vaccinations are up to date. Carry a basic first-aid kit and keep contact information for local medical facilities readily available.

Plan Ahead: Create a flexible itinerary that accommodates your family's needs. Be prepared for occasional changes and allow for downtime.

Safety Conversations: Have discussions with your children about safety measures and what to do if they become separated from you. Establish a meeting point in crowded places.

General Tips for All Travelers

Secure Travel Insurance: Irrespective of whether you're journeying solo or with your family, having travel insurance is essential. It offers peace of mind in case of unexpected situations.

Familiarize with Local Currency: Get acquainted with the local currency and maintain a mix of cash and cards for diverse expenses.

Respect Local Customs: Be respectful of local traditions and dress codes, particularly when visiting religious sites.

Stay Informed: Stay updated on the latest travel advisories and local regulations. Adhere to health and safety guidelines, especially in a post-pandemic context.

Capture Precious Memories: Document your travels through photographs and journals. These memories will be cherished for years to come.

The Balkans promise a captivating blend of history, culture, and natural wonders. Whether you're embarking on a solitary expedition or traveling with your family, these tips will help you make the most of your adventure while ensuring a safe and unforgettable experience in this remarkable region.

Printed in Great Britain
by Amazon

48845720R00086